WELBECK
CHILDREN'S BOOKS

First published in Great Britain in 2025 by Welbeck Children's Books
An imprint of Hachette Children's Group
Text © 2025 Simon Mugford
Design & Illustration © 2025 Dan Green
Text for this edition adapted by Hannah Dolan

ISBN: 978-1-80453-823-4

Dan Green and Simon Mugford have asserted their moral rights to be identified as the illustrator and author of this Work in accordance with the Copyright Designs and Patents Act 1988.

All rights reserved. This book is sold subject to the condition that it may not be reproduced, stored in a retrieval system or transmitted in any form or by any means, electronic, mechanical, photocopying, recording, or otherwise, without the publisher's prior consent.

Writer: Simon Mugford
Designer and Illustrator: Dan Green
Designer: Arvind Shah
Design Manager: Sam James
Senior Commissioning Editor: Suhel Ahmed
Production: Melanie Robertson

Printed in China
10 9 8 7 6 5 4 3 2 1

Disclaimer: All names, characters, trademarks, service marks, and trade names referred to herein are the property of their respective owners and are used solely for identification purposes. This book is a publication of Welbeck Publishing Group Limited and has not been licensed, approved, sponsored, or endorsed by any person or entity.

A CIP catalogue record for this book is available from the British Library.

Welbeck Children's Books
An imprint of Hachette Children's Group
Part of Hodder & Stoughton Limited
Carmelite House, 50 Victoria Embankment
London EC4Y 0DZ
The authorised representative in the EEA is Hachette Ireland, 8 Castlecourt Centre,
Dublin 15, D15 XTP3, Ireland (email: info@hbgi.ie)
An Hachette UK Company
www.hachette.co.uk
www.hachettechildrens.co.uk

FOOTBALL STORIES

KERR

SIMON MUGFORD

DAN GREEN

Say hello to an Australian sporting superstar! Sam Kerr is one of the greatest goalscorers ever, and she's an inspiration to young footballers around the world.

What makes Sam such an amazing player?
She's speedy, determined and brilliant at scoring goals.
Sam's also a great leader who inspires her team-mates.

Sam was born in 1993 in East Fremantle, near Perth in Australia. She lived there with her parents, Roger and Roxanne.

Sam also has three older siblings. She has a sister called Maddi, and brothers whose names are Levi and Daniel.

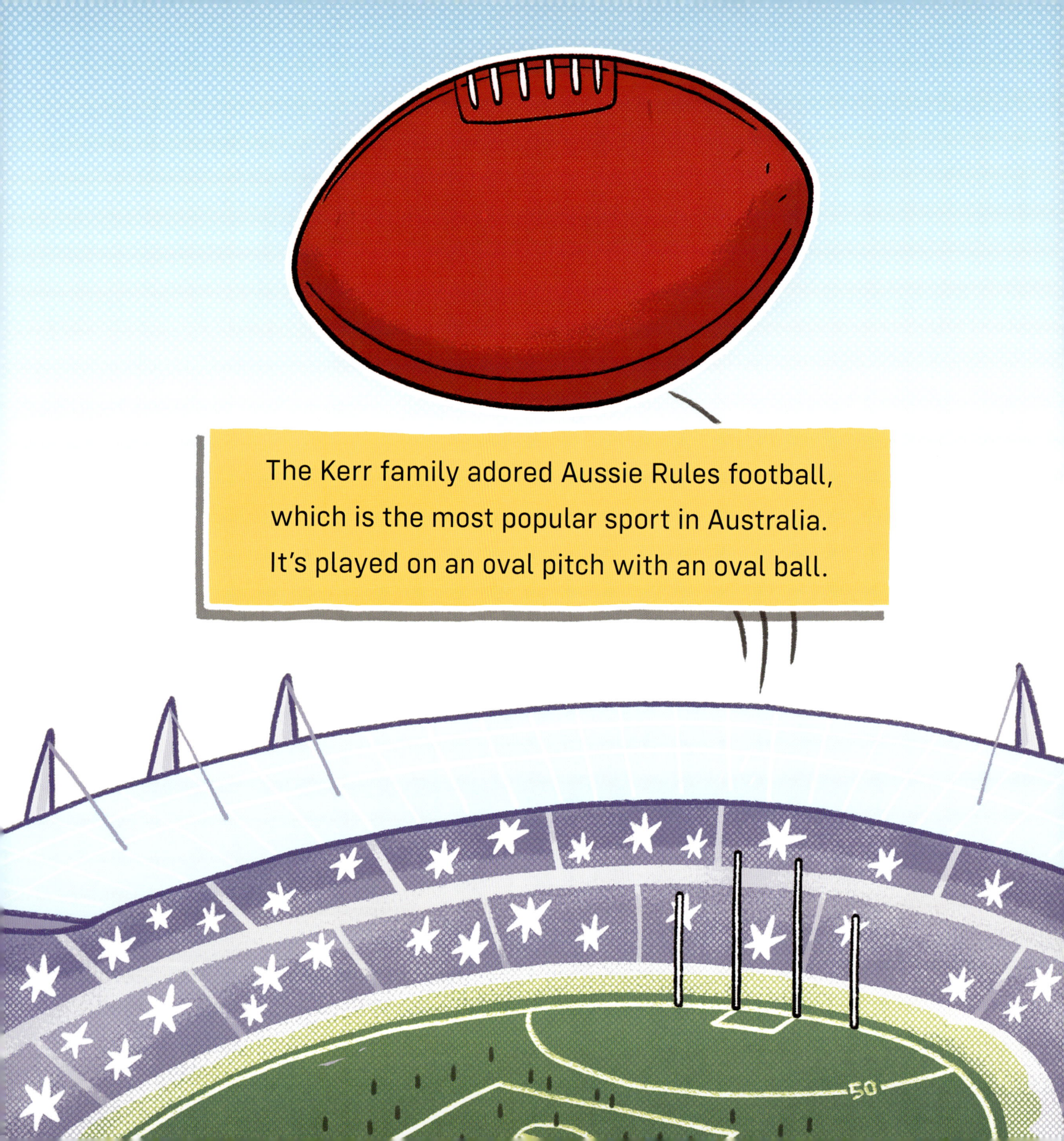

The Kerr family adored Aussie Rules football, which is the most popular sport in Australia. It's played on an oval pitch with an oval ball.

Sam's dad, Roger, played for East Fremantle, Adelaide and Perth before Sam was born.

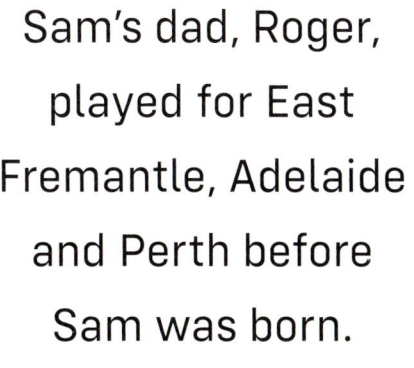

And her brother Daniel played for the West Coast Eagles.

Sam was a huge West Coast Eagles fan and part of their cheer squad.

GO EAGLES!

With so many sporty family members, it's no surprise that Sam was sports mad as a kid.

She played Aussie Rules, of course. She also played cricket and netball, and she was a brilliant runner, too.

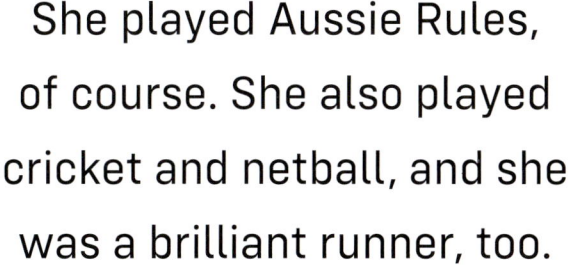

Sam even taught herself to do backflips on the school sports field! They later became her famous goal celebration.

Aussie Rules is a very tough sport with lots of contact and hard tackling like you see in rugby. When Sam was young, there were no girls' teams, so she played with the boys.

But by the time Sam was 12, the boys were getting much bigger and stronger than her, and she kept getting injured.

Sam's dad and coach told her to stop playing. She was so disappointed!

Sam's cousin, Dylan, played football with a nearby team – the Western Knights. He asked Sam to come and play.

Sam decided to give football a chance anyway.
It took a while, but once Sam started scoring
goals she began to love it (a bit)!

Sam spent three years at Western Knights learning about football and growing her skills.

One day, a talent scout came to see her play. He was very impressed. He asked Sam to try out for Perth Glory, a team in the W-League – the top women's football league in Australia.

Perth Glory snapped Sam up when they saw her play. She joined the adult team at just 15 years old!

Sam was on the road to football superstardom, and soon she was selected to play for the Matildas. That's the nickname of the Australian women's football team.

Sam still didn't totally love playing football at the time, but playing for her country made her feel very proud. She knew then that football was her game.

When Sam was 16, she played in her first big football tournament for the Matildas – the Women's Asian Cup.

Sam scored her first goal for the Matildas' first team at the tournament, and she did her first backflip goal celebration.

A goal from Sam in the final helped the team to win the tournament for the first time!

Two years later, Sam moved to the other side of the country to play for Sydney FC.

In Australia, the football season runs from October to January. When Sydney's season ended, Sam flew to the USA to play for New York Flash, whose season runs from April to August.

This was the start of a time when Sam played for two different teams on different sides of the world!

Sam spent two seasons scoring goals for Sydney FC, and she was voted Australian Women's Footballer of the Year in 2013.

Then she went back to Perth Glory for five more seasons in Australia.

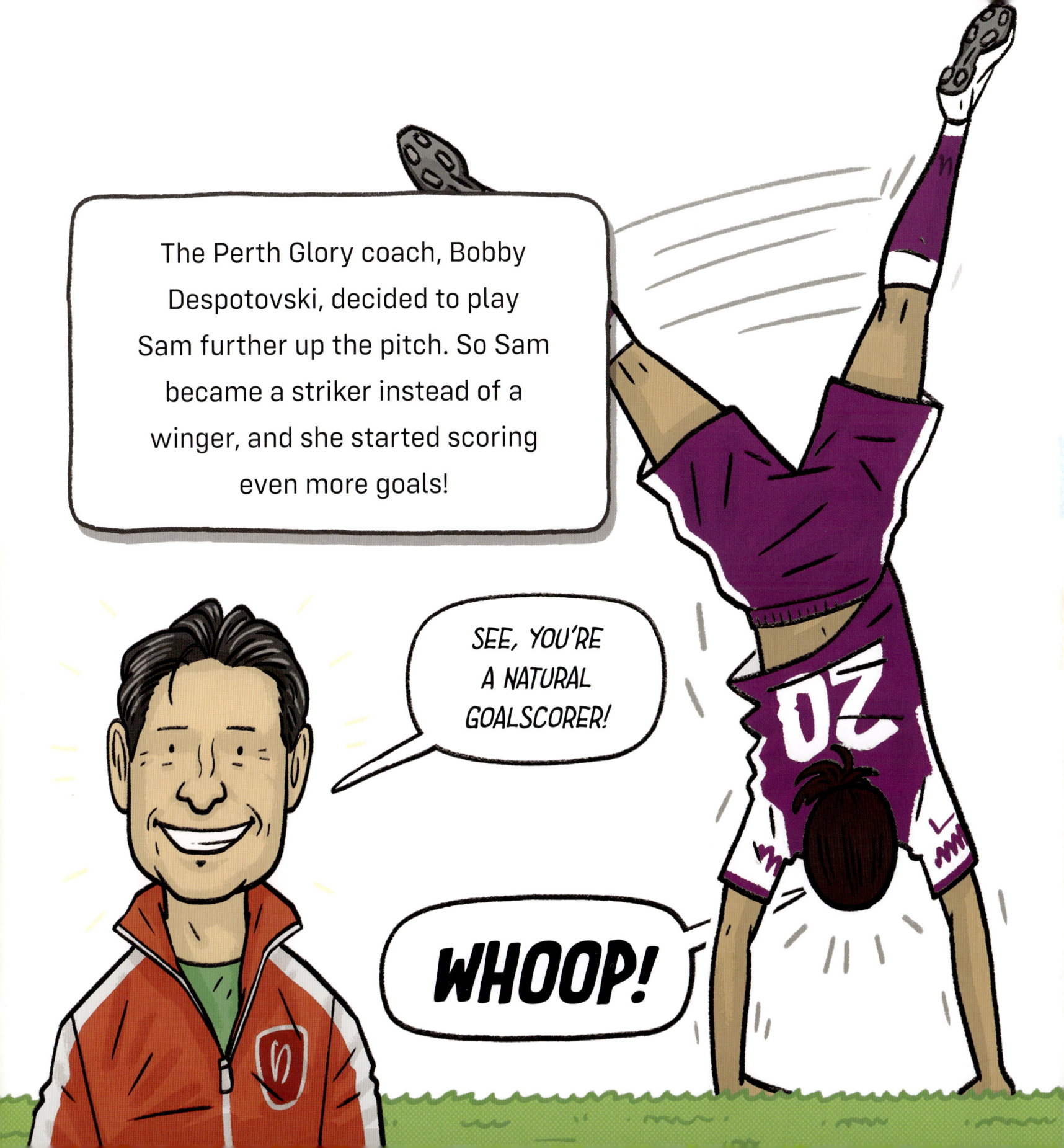

In the USA, Sam moved to Sky Blue FC in New Jersey for three seasons. Then she went to the Chicago Red Stars.

Sam was on fire! She became the top goalscorer in America's National Women's Soccer League for three seasons in a row.

The top scorer in a league or competition is given a Golden Boot trophy. Now she had three Golden Boots, plus two Golden Boots in Australia's W-League!

Sam made a big decision in 2019. She moved to England to join Chelsea! They are one of the best teams in the Women's Super League.

Sam had a tricky start at Chelsea. She was injured and she had to get used to English football, which is tough and fast.

But soon Sam found her groove and started scoring lots of goals. She won another Golden Boot and helped Chelsea win three big trophies!

Sam was a star player for Australia, too, and she was named the Matildas's captain in 2019.

She helped the team reach the quarter-finals of the World Cup in 2015, and the semi-finals in 2023.